Read This...® On Our ♥ Anniversary

A GUIDED JOURNAL
CELEBRATING
A LONG,
HAPPY
LIFE TOGETHER

By Christy Howard & Annie Presley

Read This…® On Our Anniversary
by Christy Howard & Annie Presley

Fifth Edition

Printed in the United States of America

ISBN: 978-0-9985598-8-9

www.BooksByACE.com

Cover and book design: Frank M. Addington

Other books in the series include: Read This...® When I'm Dead,
Read This...® On Your Birthday & Read This...® About My House

ACE Publishing, LLC
KANSAS CITY, MO

Welcome to the Story of Your Life...Together

The purpose of this book is to give you the chance to capture the "spark" of your happy life together. Focus on the goal. Build on it. Enjoy and celebrate each other! Throughout this book, Christy and Annie share their thoughts and ideas to inspire you.

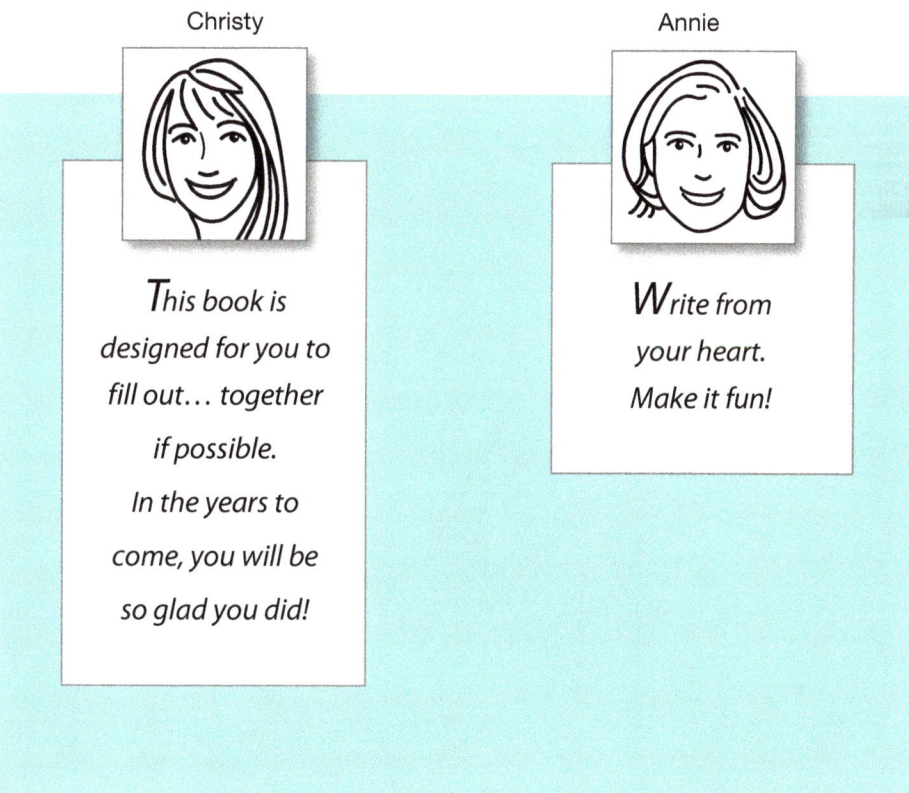

Christy

*This book is designed for you to fill out... together if possible.
In the years to come, you will be so glad you did!*

Annie

Write from your heart. Make it fun!

This Book Contains Information About Us

_____

NAME & NAME

_____

_____

_____

_____

ADDRESS

_____

DATE

CONTENTS

INTRODUCTION

What it takes to be a successful, happy, loving couple over decades together looks different for each couple. This book is YOURS. It provides the framework for you to begin talking to each other about what you can both do to help make your relationship strong and happy. It is meant to be a tool, a window for you both to look through as your life together changes before your eyes.

Most of us spend time thinking about our vows well ahead of time. Then the big day is over and life begins. But what did we say? What should we have said? What did we forget?

That is where this book comes in. You have a chance to reflect on your life with your partner. It provides a framework for you to look back and then look forward — together.

Businesses do this all the time. It's how to keep on track, or decide to modify the track so things can run more smoothly. Consider thinking of your relationship as a business whose purpose is to love each other better every year!

Hello • Hola • Bonjo
• Aloha • Ciao • Hau
Hallo • Salud • Bol
Hej • Ola • Hi • Selam
Xin Chao • Namast
• Bwanji • Guten • Tag
Goddag • Aniin • Mor
• Siema • Sawubona
Hello • Hola • Bonjo
• Aloha • Ciao • Hau
Hallo • Salud • Bol
Hej • Ola • Hi • Selam
Xin Chao • Namast
• Bwanji • Guten Tag
Goddag • Aniin Mor
• Siema • Sawubona
Hello • Hola • Bonjo

How We Met and Decided to Spend Our Lives Together

You entered my life and changed my world forever.

H O W   W E   F I R S T   M E T

I remember thinking

And I thought you were

I remember thinking

And I thought you were

OUR ROMANCE

I knew I wanted to spend my life with you when

I knew I wanted to spend my life with you when

The Proposal

Some proposals are planned. Some are spontaneous where two people just decide to take the plunge. However yours came about, it is yours and that makes it special!

BEYOND THE VOWS

Our Ceremony and the First Year

The warmth of your presence brings me a sense of calm.

Our Ceremony

Insert Photo of Ceremony

Date   Time   Location

These Were Our Vows

We Chose These Vows Because

Consider renewing your commitment annually. My neighbors do it and they just celebrated 50 years together!

Our Honeymoon

We Chose This Because

Our Best Honeymoon Memories

Whether you went on a trip anywhere is not really the point. The honeymoon is really the beginning of something — so just explain where or how you spent those first weeks of your life together.

How You Might Want To Treat Each Other During this First Year

This section is important because daily life is what often surprises us. It isn't exciting. It is hard work. You get tired, the bills need to be paid, and extended families and friends have expectations of your time. You transition from being the "engaged couple" who everyone celebrates and congratulates to being part of the fabric of society. Are there things you want to say to each other daily? Are there things you would like to do for each other? Are there things you would like NOT to do?

*If you have not yet read **The Five Love Languages** by Gary Chapman, go to www.5lovelanguages.com and take the quiz. You will likely find some pretty valuable information!*

What we would like to do for each other this year:

Family Mission

You are a FAMILY now. Whether you are young or old, have brought children into the relationship, will be having children, or will never have children… you are now a FAMILY.

Our First Family Mission Statement

Your family mission will likely change over time, but don't worry about that now. Draft the family mission that fits your family today.

Is there a couple who has been together for a long time whose interactions you would like to emulate? Look ahead and keep your eye on where you want to take your relationship!

Ten or Twenty Years from Today:

Jump forward from today. Where do you see your relationship in 10 or even 20 years? What will it look like?

10 years

20 years

Three

Our Early Anniversaries

I am proud of the "we" we have come to be.

Our First
Anniversary

How we celebrated

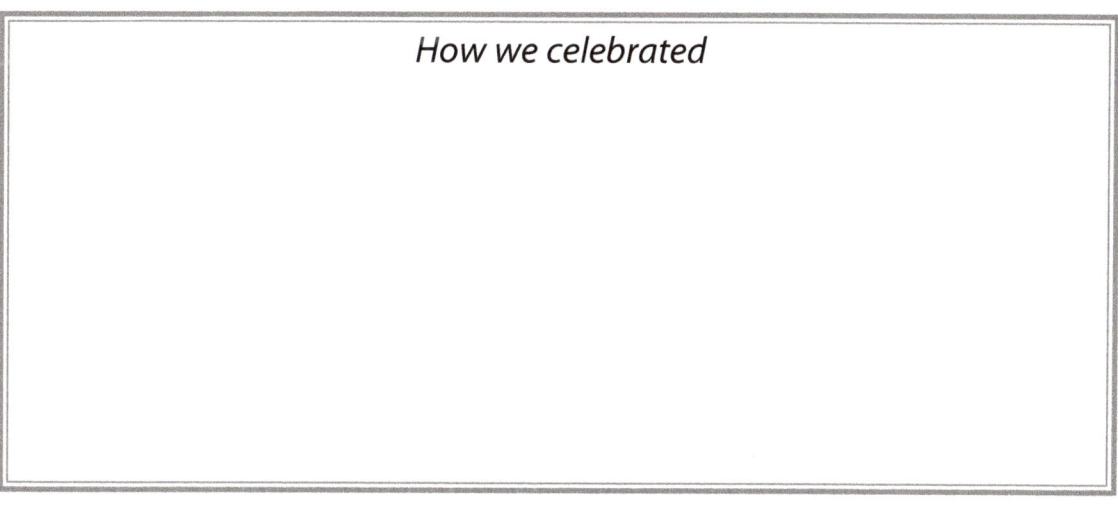

The BEST memories of this year (events, trips, experiences):

What we learned about each other this year:

Our First Anniversary

Our goals for the coming year:

Things we would like to do together:

How we would like to interact to enhance our relationship:

WARM THOUGHTS

I love your

I love your

Be sure to identify who is writing the response in each box. You will enjoy looking back at this one day.

Talking to you makes those difficult times better and makes everything good that much sweeter.

Our Second
Anniversary

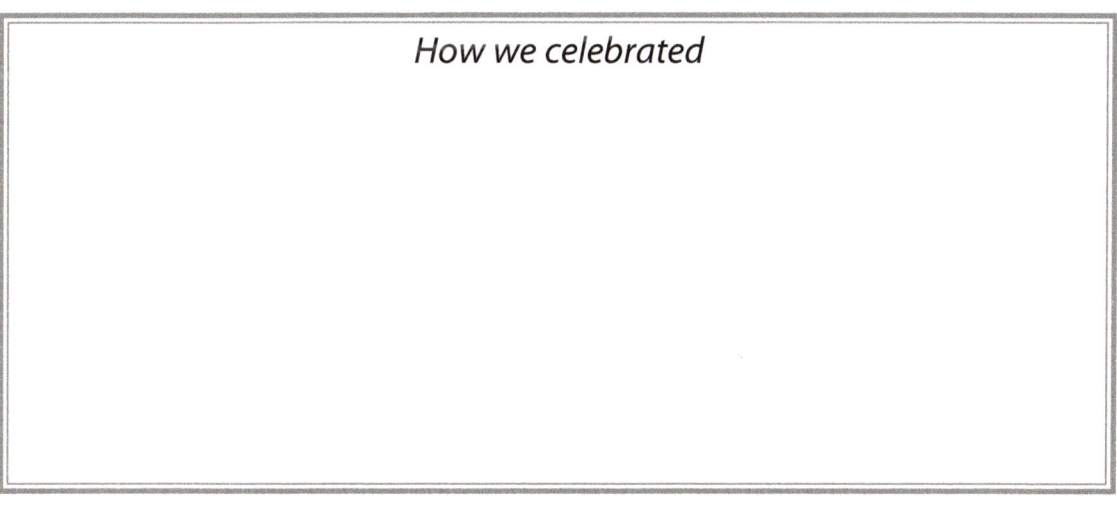

How we celebrated

The BEST memories of this year (events, trips, experiences):

What we learned about each other this year:

Our Second Anniversary

Our goals for the coming year:

Things we would like to do together:

How we would like to interact to enhance our relationship:

Have you thought about planning a surprise or making a romantic gesture? We often take the time to surprise each other while dating. Remember those surprises and kind gestures make us feel special and remain important over the years.

Sharing life with you is the best part of my life.

Our Third

Anniversary

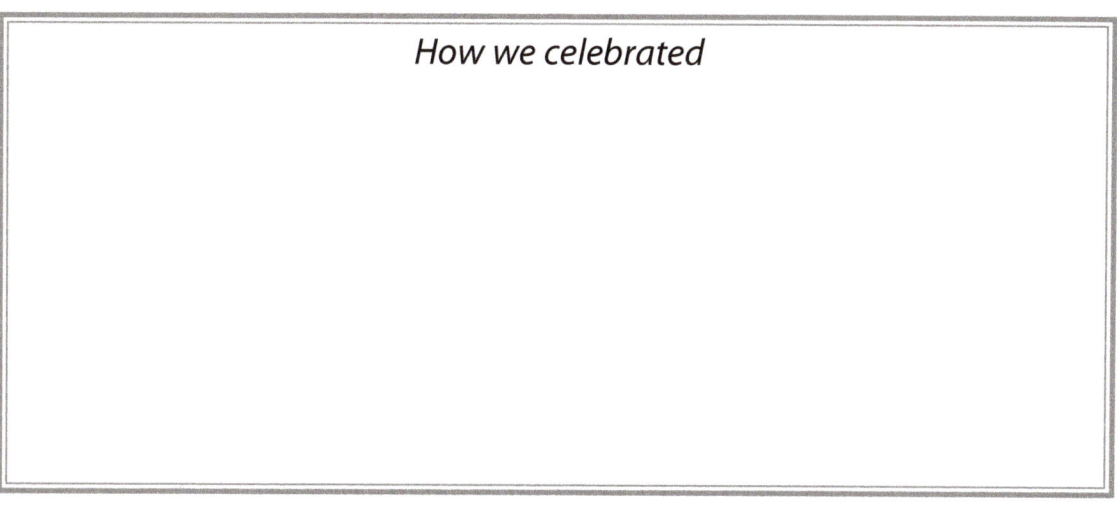

How we celebrated

The BEST memories of this year (events, trips, experiences):

What we learned about each other this year:

Our Third

Anniversary

Our goals for the coming year:

Things we would like to do together:

How we would like to interact to enhance our relationship:

WARM THOUGHTS

I love the way you smile when you are

I love the way you smile when you are

Is it when you are playing with the dogs or when you are watching your favorite sports team, or planting in the garden? Or maybe it is when you are water skiing or riding a horse…

When we walk together I can feel your presence – even when we are silent.

Our Fourth
Anniversary

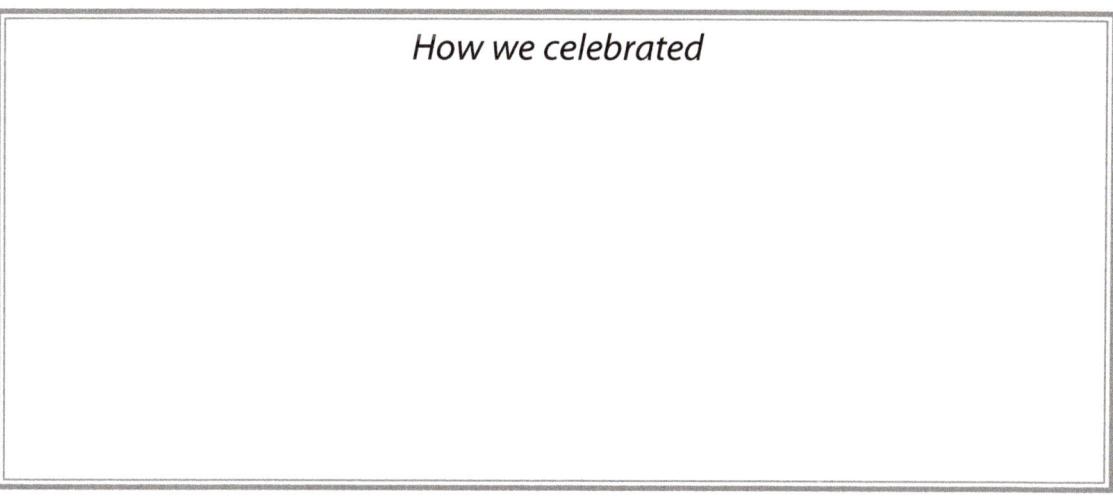

How we celebrated

The BEST memories of this year (events, trips, experiences):

What we learned about each other this year:

Learning about each other helps your understanding of each other increase.

Our Fourth Anniversary

Our goals for the coming year:

Things we would like to do together:

How we would like to interact to enhance our relationship:

WARM THOUGHTS

You always make me laugh when you

You always make me laugh when you

Be sure to remember what makes you laugh. Perhaps laughter IS the best medicine!

I love knowing you are in the next room.

Our Fifth
Anniversary

How we celebrated

The BEST memories of this year (events, trips, experiences):

What we learned about each other this year:

Our Fifth
Anniversary

Our goals for the coming year:

Things we would like to do together:

How we would like to interact to enhance our relationship:

W A R M   T H O U G H T S

One of my favorite memories is when we

One of my favorite memories is when we

Remember you are a team. Did you solve a problem together, do something silly together, or do something warm and kind for someone else? All these things help build your relationship.

When you call me, I am reminded how lucky we are to have each other.

Our Sixth
Anniversary

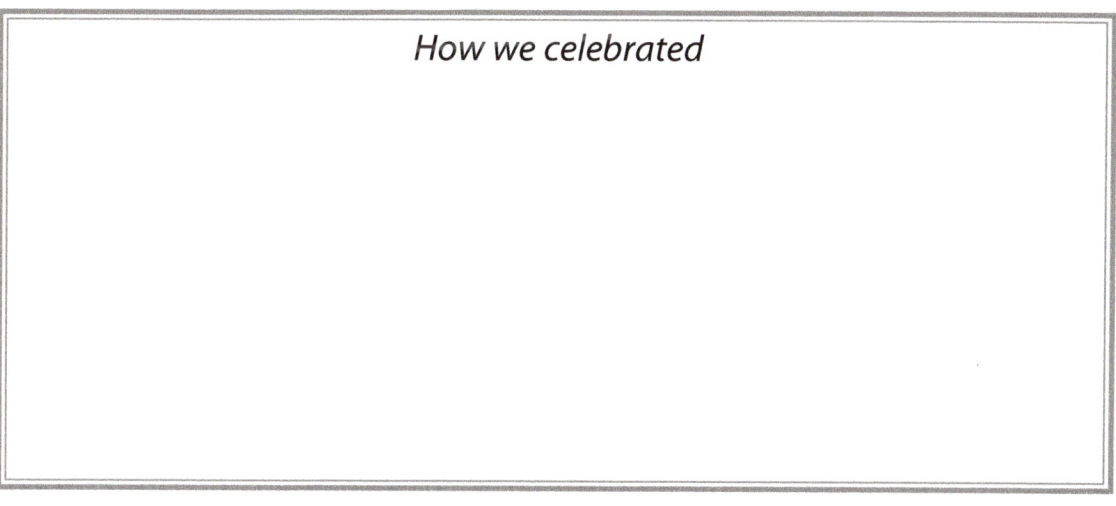

How we celebrated

The BEST memories of this year (events, trips, experiences):

What we learned about each other this year:

Our Sixth Anniversary

Our goals for the coming year:

Things we would like to do together:

How we would like to interact to enhance our relationship:

W A R M   T H O U G H T S

If we could go visit any place in the world,

I'd love to go to _____ with you so

we could _____ together.

You are here to help each other. You are a team. Think about what you can do to make your team stronger, happier, more comfortable. You are still at the beginning of this amazing journey!

If we could go visit any place in the world,

I'd love to go to _____ with you so

we could _____ together.

When you answer the phone, I know you are glad I called.

Our Seventh
Anniversary

How we celebrated

The BEST memories of this year (events, trips, experiences):

What we learned about each other this year:

Our Seventh
Anniversary

Our goals for the coming year:

Things we would like to do together:

How we would like to interact to enhance our relationship:

WARM THOUGHTS

I remember eating at _____ *with you because of the*

I remember eating at _____ *with you because of the*

Sometimes you just need to ask, "What can I do to make this a great day"?

Shopping for something little for you makes me smile.

Our Eighth
Anniversary

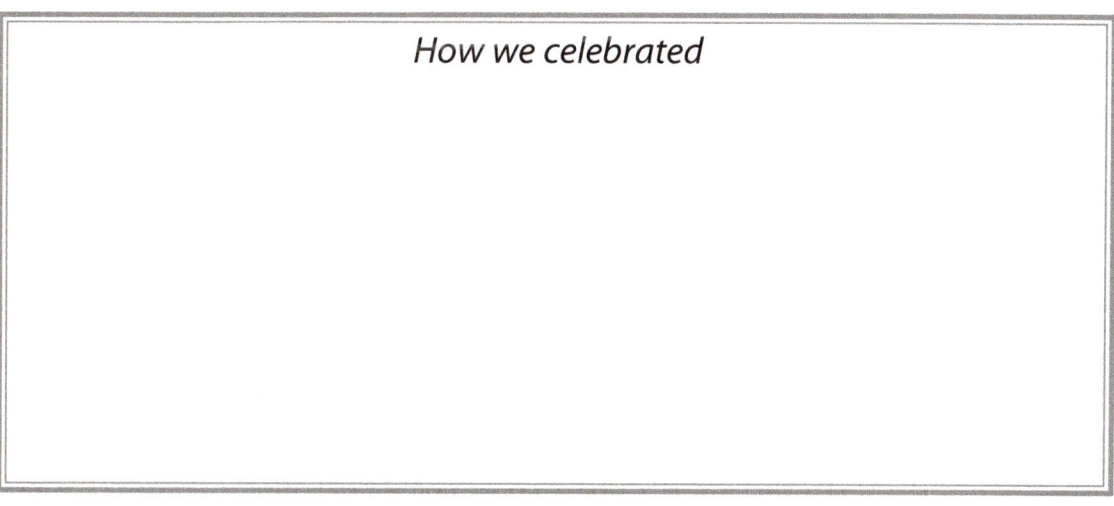

How we celebrated

The BEST memories of this year (events, trips, experiences):

What we learned about each other this year:

Our Eighth
Anniversary

Our goals for the coming year:

Things we would like to do together:

How we would like to interact to enhance our relationship:

WARM THOUGHTS

We always have fun when we watch _____

together because

We always have fun when we watch _____

together because

*L*eave little love
notes for each
other. Just in case
life gets too hectic.

I feel honored when I know you have bought something for me that you thought I would like.

Our Ninth
Anniversary

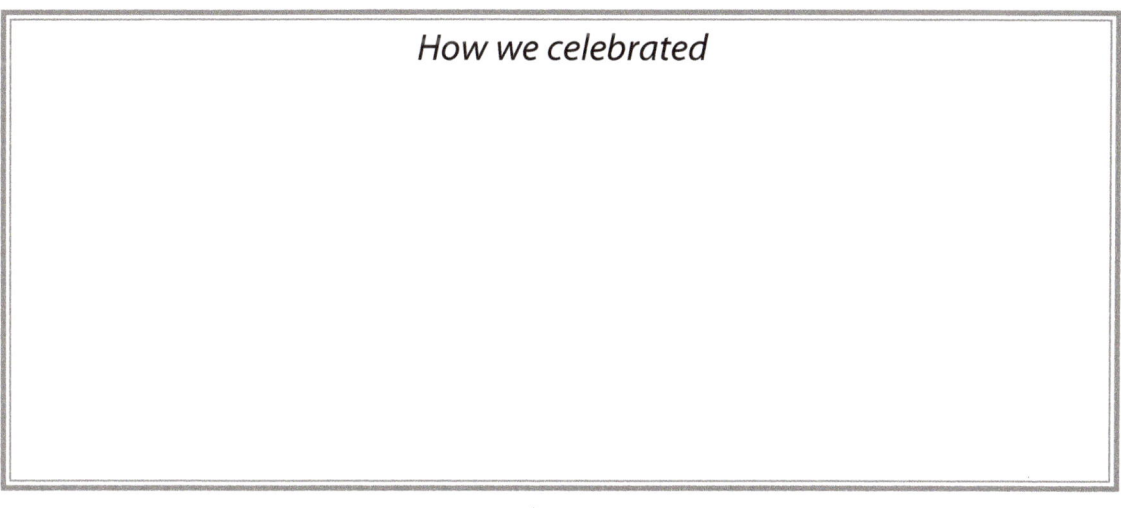

How we celebrated

The BEST memories of this year (events, trips, experiences):

What we learned about each other this year:

Our Ninth
Anniversary

Our goals for the coming year:

Things we would like to do together:

How we would like to interact to enhance our relationship:

W A R M   T H O U G H T S

I hope we get to go see _____

because

Staycations count too! You know, the time you take off and never leave home. They can be fun if you plan them together – like you would plan a trip away.

I hope we get to go see _____

because

You make me feel like I am special. Thank you for that.

Our Tenth
Anniversary

Congratulations on your 10th anniversary!

How we celebrated

The BEST memories of this year (events, trips, experiences):

What we learned about each other this year:

For fun look at page 25 to see what you thought on your first anniversary.

Our Tenth Anniversary

Our goals for the coming year:

Things we would like to do together:

How we would like to interact to enhance our relationship:

W A R M   T H O U G H T S

I wish I had saved the note you wrote me when

I wish I had saved the note you wrote me when

Leave a note for each other in the seat of the car! A fun surprise!

Congratulations
on 10 years Together!

Now is the time to look back and forward.

I'm glad we are together because

Actively find little ways to make each day better for your partner. Celebrate your special relationship!

I'm glad we are together because

Our List of Big Changes

You are both ten years older than you were when you wrote your first Family Mission. Even if that is the only thing that changed, it is time for a rewrite!

Updated Family Mission Statement

If there are additional family members, be sure to have them provide input to the new mission.

See page 21 for your first Family Mission Statement.

Our Journey Toward 20 Years Together

Our Eleventh
Anniversary

How we celebrated

The BEST memories of this year (events, trips, experiences):

Our goals for the coming year:

WARM THOUGHTS

The car I drove when we met was a

Now I drive

Ask friends and family members to reminisce with you about fun you've had together.

The car I drove when we met was a

Now I drive

Our Twelfth
Anniversary

How we celebrated

The BEST memories of this year (events, trips, experiences):

Our goals for the coming year:

WARM THOUGHTS

My favorite thing about our first house was the _____

because

My favorite thing about our first house was the _____

because

Build on those happy memories. They help create a fabulous foundation!

Our Thirteenth
Anniversary

How we celebrated

The BEST memories of this year (events, trips, experiences):

Our goals for the coming year:

WARM THOUGHTS

I liked learning how to _____ with you.

I liked learning how to _____ with you.

When you learn something together, you are achieving something together… whether the learning is fun and easy or difficult.

Our Fourteenth
Anniversary

How we celebrated

The BEST memories of this year (events, trips, experiences):

Our goals for the coming year:

WARM THOUGHTS

I was proud when you

I was proud when you

It is all too easy to forget to tell your loved ones you are proud of them. Remember to tell your partner all the good things you tell other people about them!

The world is filled with memories of us at every turn . . . and those are my favorite memories.

Our Fifteenth
Anniversary

How we celebrated

The BEST memories of this year (events, trips, experiences):

What we learned about each other this year:

Our Fifteenth

Our goals for the coming years:

Things we would like to do together:

How we would like to interact to enhance our relationship:

WARM THOUGHTS

I love that you are very _____

because

I love that you are very _____

because

*U*se adjectives or descriptive words. Funny, loyal, smart, frugal, generous, organized, patient, inclusive, fashionable, relaxed, happy, strong…
The list is endless!
The "because" is what really matters!

Our Sixteenth
Anniversary

How we celebrated

The BEST memories of this year (events, trips, experiences):

Our goals for the coming year:

W A R M   T H O U G H T S

I remember holding hands at

Holding hands is a very warm gesture. Take time to hold hands. Slow down together. If you have fallen out of practice, reach out… and reach back!

I remember holding hands at

Our Seventeenth
Anniversary

How we celebrated

The BEST memories of this year (events, trips, experiences):

Our goals for the coming year:

W A R M   T H O U G H T S

We laughed hard when we were

Laughter really does have a positive impact on us. Remembering times of laughter is such a good, happy experience!

We laughed hard when we were

Our Eighteenth
Anniversary

How we celebrated

The BEST memories of this year (events, trips, experiences):

Our goals for the coming year:

WARM THOUGHTS

I'd like to have another date night with you

like we did when we

I'd like to have another date night with you

like we did when we

Maybe it was recent or maybe it was long ago. Remember it and then plan something else fun — or repeat that date!

Our Nineteenth
Anniversary

How we celebrated

The BEST memories of this year (events, trips, experiences):

Our goals for the coming year:

WARM THOUGHTS

My favorite vacation memory is

My favorite vacation memory is

If you didn't take a photo of it, just your description will bring it back to life!

The joy I feel is more than doubled when I share it with you.

Our Twentieth
Anniversary

Congratulations on your 20th Anniversary!

How we celebrated

The BEST memories of this year (events, trips, experiences):

For fun look back at page 25 to see what you thought 20 years ago!

What we learned about each other this year:

Our Twentieth Anniversary

Our goals for the coming year:

Things we would like to do together:

How we would like to interact to enhance our relationship:

WARM THOUGHTS

Big congratulations on another major achievement! Time to celebrate each other!

I want to remember how we

I want to remember how we

What are the best things about your relationship? What do others see? Help give other people something positive to emulate as they begin their committed lives together.

Congratulations
on 20 years Together!

Now is the time to look back and forward.

I'm glad I chose to spend my life with you because

I'm glad I chose to spend my life with you because

Our List of Big Changes

If family members have moved out on their own, that impacts how you all interact, too! See your 10th Anniversary for your last Family Mission Statement on page 65.

Updated Family Mission Statement

Twenty years is a long journey! Life has definitely changed both inside and outside your home. Technology may even impact how you interact! What matters is your commitment and your kindness toward each other.

Our Journey Toward 50 Years Together

Our Twenty-First
Anniversary

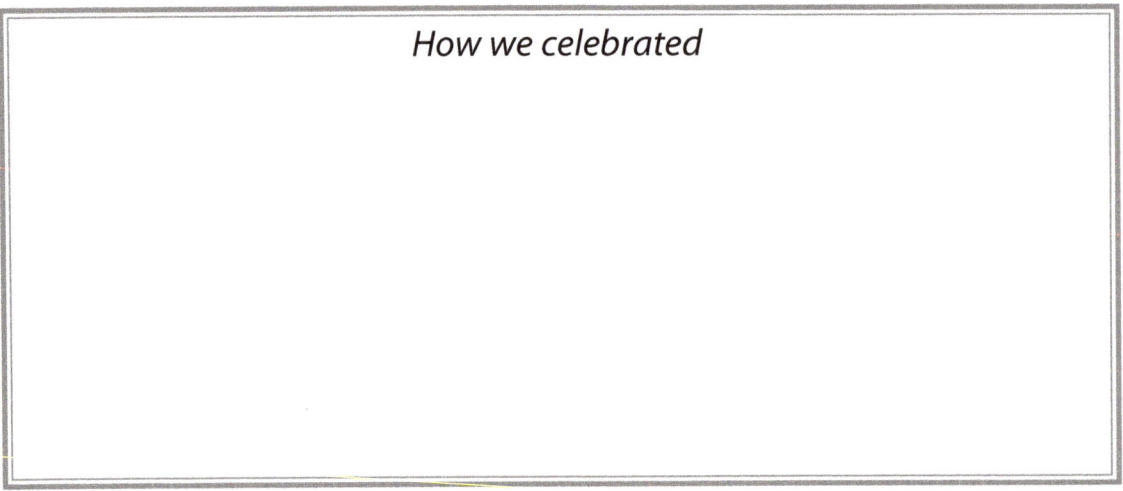

How we celebrated

The BEST memories of this year (events, trips, experiences):

Our goals for the coming year:

WARM THOUGHTS

Our favorite car was _____

because

Our favorite car was _____

because

Your favorites do not need to be the same. It can be fun to continue to learn little things about each other that are unexpected.

Our Twenty-Second

Anniversary

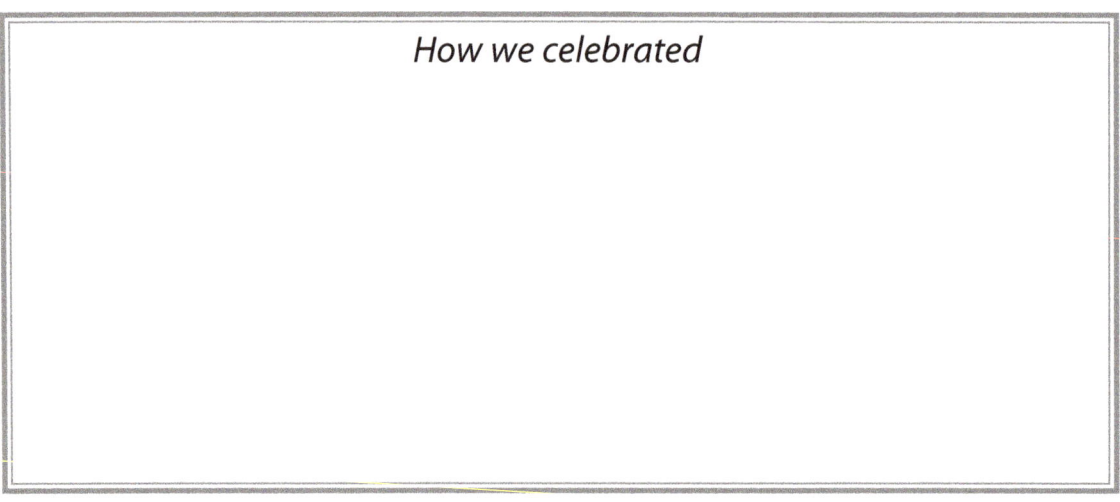

How we celebrated

The BEST memories of this year (events, trips, experiences):

Our goals for the coming year:

WARM THOUGHTS

I was excited to introduce you to _____

because

Bringing together people you love is always memorable.

I was excited to introduce you to _____

because

Our Twenty-Third
Anniversary

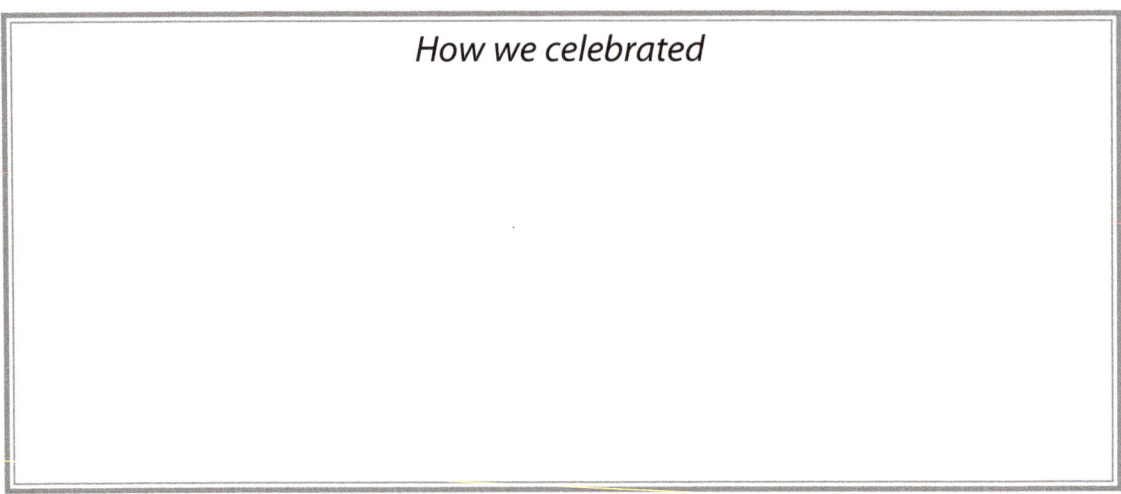

How we celebrated

The BEST memories of this year (events, trips, experiences):

Our goals for the coming year:

WARM THOUGHTS

I love how you always remember to

I love how you always remember to

Is it that your loved one always says please or sends you flowers or unloads the dishwasher or calls their sister or wrestles with the puppy? What makes you smile?

Our Twenty-Fourth
Anniversary

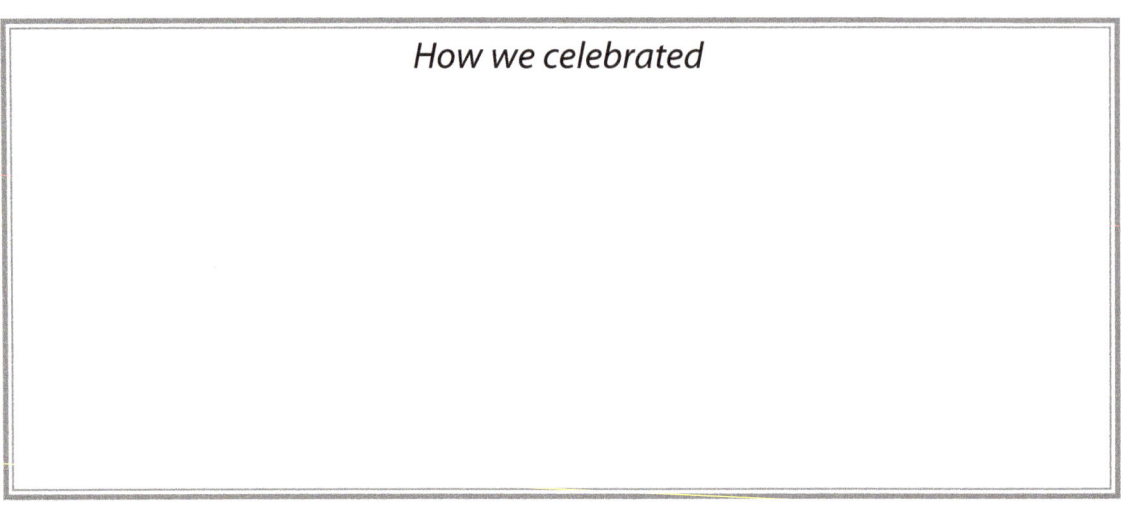

How we celebrated

The BEST memories of this year (events, trips, experiences):

Our goals for the coming year:

WARM THOUGHTS

Our favorite movie treats are

Our favorite movie treats are

Treats at home for movies or "out" at a theatre may be different. Treats change over time. When you look back at this some day, these treats may no loner exist.

Together we are so much stronger than each of us is alone.

Our Twenty-Fifth
Anniversary

How we celebrated

The BEST memories of this year (events, trips, experiences):

What we learned about each other this year:

Our Twenty-Fifth
Anniversary

Our goals for the coming years:

Things we would like to do together:

How we would like to interact to enhance our relationship:

W A R M   T H O U G H T S

I first knew I wanted to spend my life

with you when we were

I first knew I wanted to spend my life

with you when we were

This is a happy memory that may have "dawned" on you at different times and places. Or it may have happened at the same moment.

Our Twenty-Sixth
Anniversary

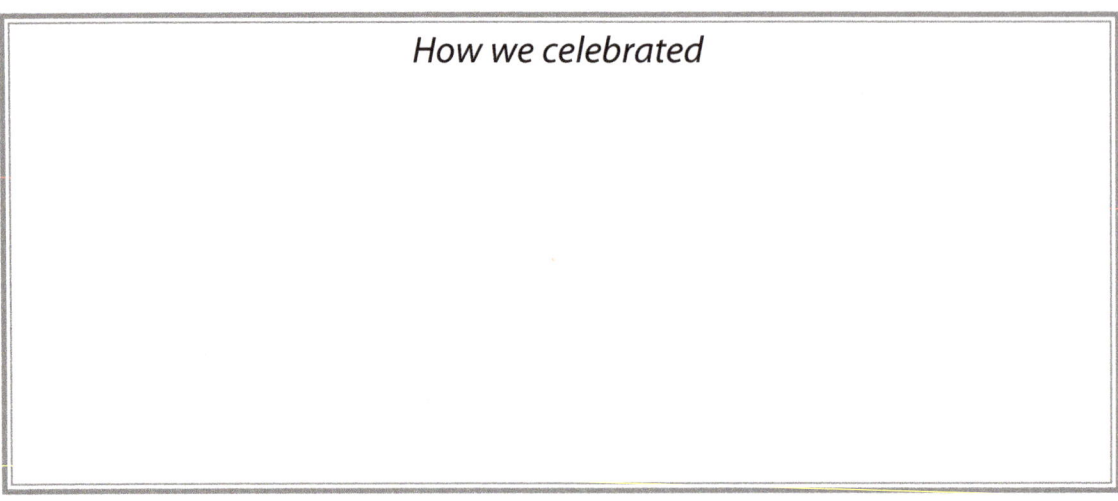

How we celebrated

The BEST memories of this year (events, trips, experiences):

Our goals for the coming year:

WARM THOUGHTS

You have the best taste in

We are all different and those strengths help "fill" relationships. Taste in music, clothes, food decorating, vacation plans, books, movies, shoes... There are so many choices!

You have the best taste in

Our Twenty-Seventh
Anniversary

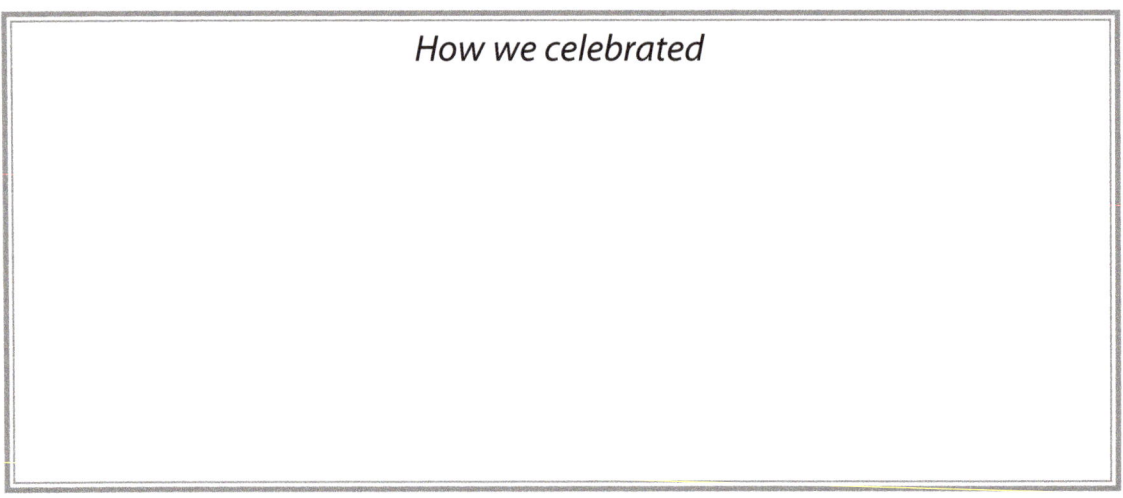

How we celebrated

The BEST memories of this year (events, trips, experiences):

Our goals for the coming year:

W A R M   T H O U G H T S

I remember the time we bought _____ (flavor)

ice cream because

Do you remember ordering or buying the same flavor of ice cream? Have your favorite flavors changed over time?

I remember the time we bought _____ (flavor)

ice cream because

READ THIS...® ON OUR ANNIVERSARY

111

Our Twenty-Eighth
Anniversary

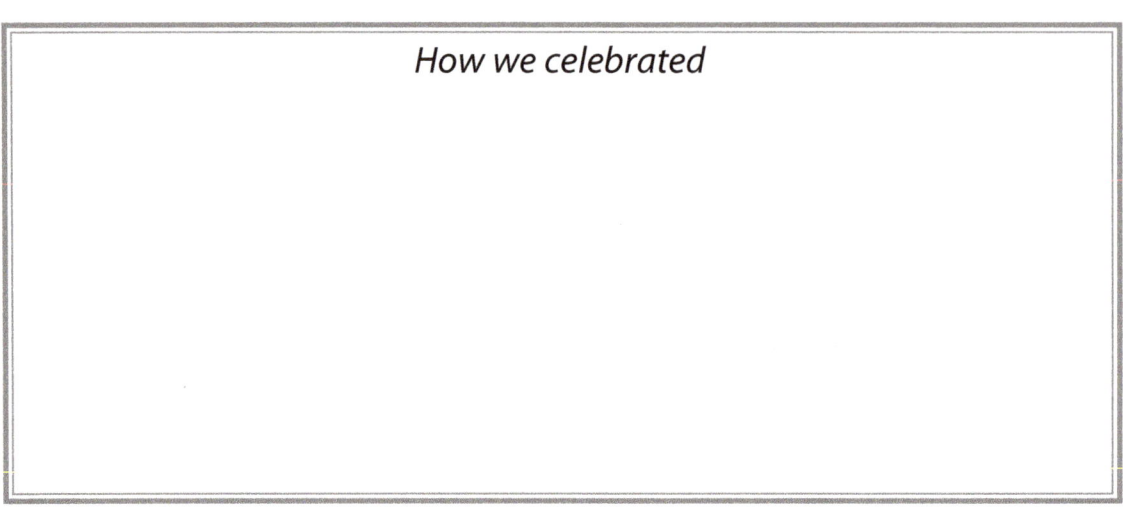

How we celebrated

The BEST memories of this year (events, trips, experiences):

Our goals for the coming year:

WARM THOUGHTS

If our life were a dance, it would be

the _____ *because*

If our life were a dance, it would be

the _____ *because*

Dances are full of expression. Is it the tango or the bump, or the swim or the waltz? Could it be the hula? Be sure to explain WHY!

Our Twenty-Ninth
Anniversary

How we celebrated

The BEST memories of this year (events, trips, experiences):

Our goals for the coming year:

WARM THOUGHTS

We used to eat _____, but we now eat

_____ because

It is quite likely that after 29 years your food choices have changed.

We used to eat _____, but we now eat

_____ because

Recalling the early days of our relationship makes me happy.

Our Thirtieth
Anniversary

How we celebrated

The BEST memories of this year (events, trips, experiences):

Our goals for the coming year:

Our Thirtieth Anniversary

Our goals for the coming year:

Things we would like to do together:

How we would like to interact to enhance our relationship:

W A R M   T H O U G H T S

My favorite story to tell people about us is when we

Sharing special stories about your life can help you bond and can enhance your sense of "team."

My favorite story to tell people about us is when we

Congratulations
on 30 years Together!

Now is the time to look back and forward.

I'm glad I chose to spend my life with you because

I'm glad I chose to spend my life with you because

Our List of Big Changes

You are both ten years older than you were when you wrote your last Family Mission Statement. Even if that is the only thing that has changed, it is time for a rewrite!

Updated Family Mission Statement

If there are additional family members, be sure to have them provide input to the new mission. See your 20th Anniversary for your latest Family Mission Statement on page 93.

Our Thirty-First
Anniversary

How we celebrated

The BEST memories of this year (events, trips, experiences):

Our goals for the coming year:

WARM THOUGHTS

You were so sweet when you

Being kind is so important, and it really matters to your partner!

You were so sweet when you

Our Thirty-Second
Anniversary

How we celebrated

The BEST memories of this year (events, trips, experiences):

What we learned about each other this year:

W A R M   T H O U G H T S

The funniest thing we have done lately is

Laughter is healthy and brings joy to your soul!

The funniest thing we have done lately is

Our Thirty-Third
Anniversary

How we celebrated

The BEST memories of this year (events, trips, experiences):

Our goals for the coming year:

WARM THOUGHTS

I never get tired of your

I never get tired of your

Is it your partner's voice, smile, a special dish they prepare? Is it their calming influence or their laughter? Or their ability to tell stories?

Our Thirty-Fourth
Anniversary

How we celebrated

The BEST memories of this year (events, trips, experiences):

Our goals for the coming year:

W A R M   T H O U G H T S

My favorite color on you is _____ because

Does it remind you of a special event or does it just look good on your partner?

My favorite color on you is _____ because

I remember when we bought matching shirts. And shoes.

Our Thirty-Fifth
Anniversary

How we celebrated

The BEST memories of this year (events, trips, experiences):

What we learned about each other this year:

Our Thirty-Fifth

Anniversary

Our goals for the coming years:

Things we would like to do together:

How we would like to interact to enhance our relationship:

WARM THOUGHTS

You make the best

Is it food or is it a craft or a quality (listener, entertainer, teacher)?

You make the best

Our Thirty-Sixth
Anniversary

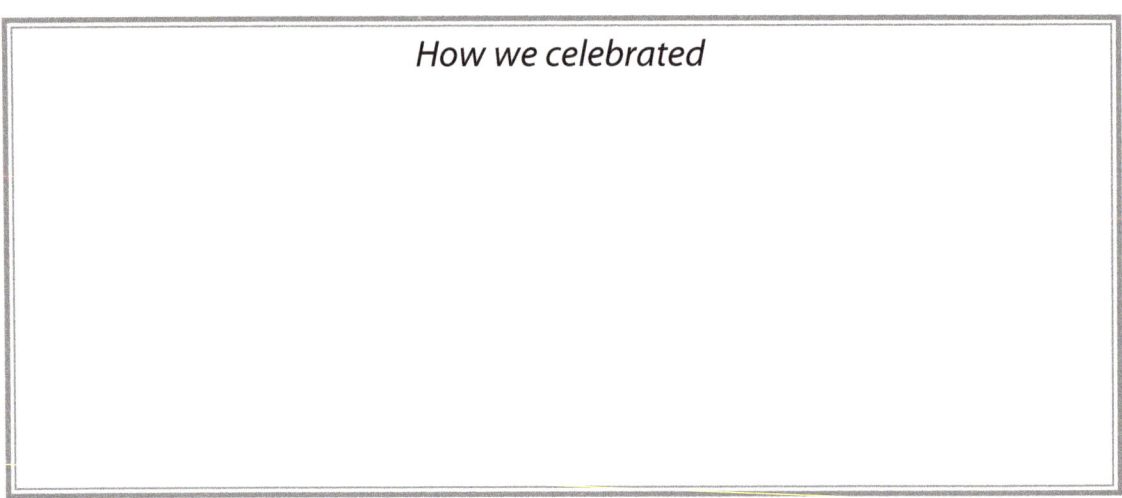

How we celebrated

The BEST memories of this year (events, trips, experiences):

Our goals for the coming year:

W A R M   T H O U G H T S

I love going to _____ together because

I love going to _____ together because

Plan your "best day" with your spouse – for fun. Just plan a day of fun activities together!

Our Thirty-Seventh
Anniversary

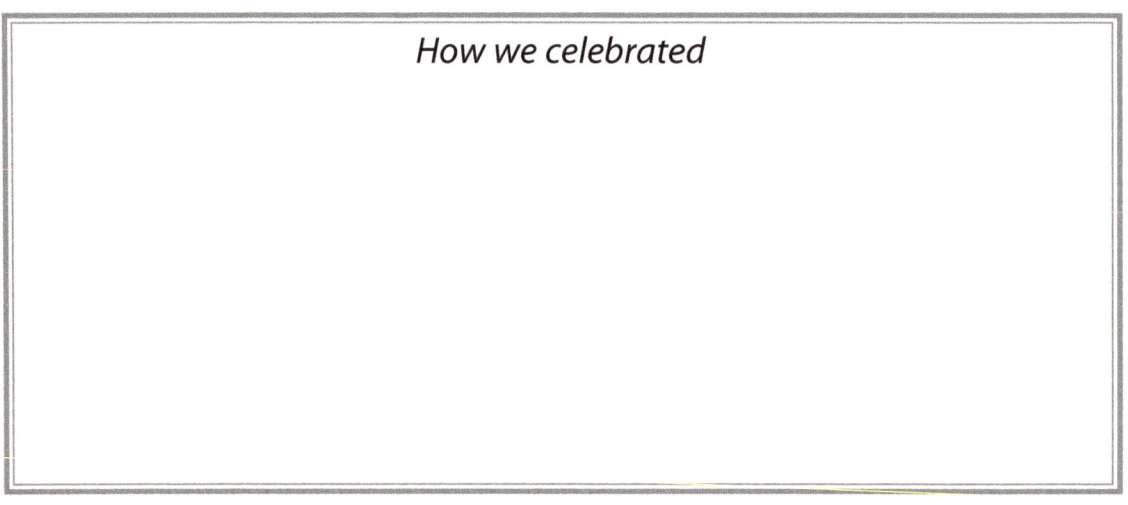

How we celebrated

The BEST memories of this year (events, trips, experiences):

Our goals for the coming year:

WARM THOUGHTS

You deserve the award for Best _____

because you

You deserve the award for Best _____

because you

I made my mom a "Best Mom" plaque when I was young. On it I listed all the things she did well. She kept it her whole life. What would you list about your partner? Kind words matter!

Our Thirty-Eighth
Anniversary

How we celebrated

The BEST memories of this year (events, trips, experiences):

Our goals for the coming year:

WARM THOUGHTS

I appreciate your advice on

I appreciate your advice on

Is it advice about something fun or handling personal matters with friends or family or work/business?

Our Thirty-Ninth
Anniversary

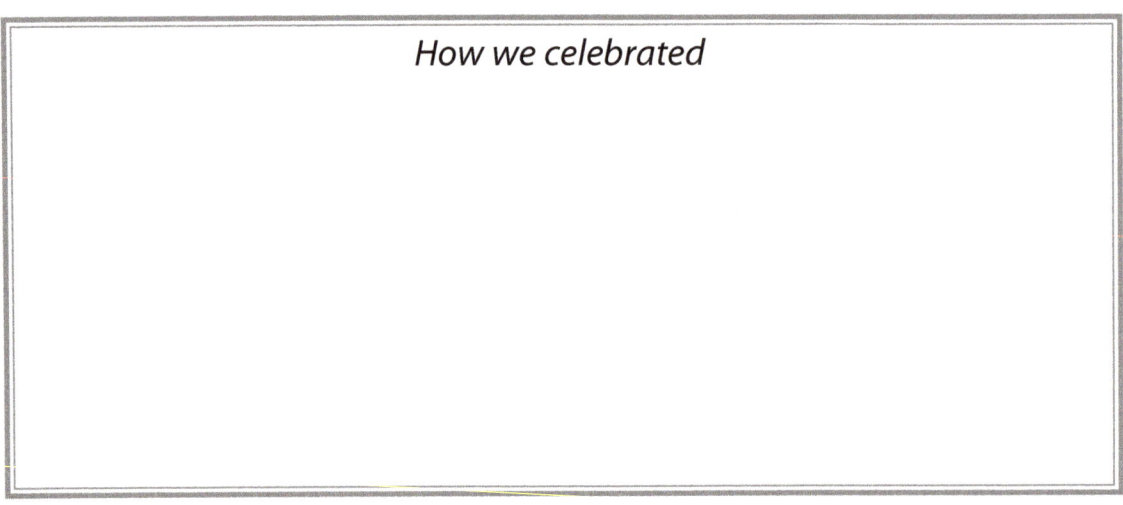

How we celebrated

The BEST memories of this year (events, trips, experiences):

Our goals for the coming year:

W A R M   T H O U G H T S

If I could plan one magical day with you,
I'd want to do these things together:

Maybe this will just be a dream, or maybe you will find a way to make it a reality. Dreaming matters.

If I could plan one magical day with you,
I'd want to do these things together:

I remember the first time I saw you. Now I know that was the minute my life changed in the very best way.

Our Fortieth
Anniversary

How we celebrated

The BEST memories of this year (events, trips, experiences):

What we learned about each other this year:

Our Fortieth
Anniversary

Our goals for the coming year:

Things we would like to do together:

How we would like to interact to enhance our relationship:

WARM THOUGHTS

I'd like to be more like you in this way

Consider your partner's behavior that you really like… the way he/she whistles, writes little poems, remembers names, tells jokes, etc.

I'd like to be more like you in this way

Congratulations
on 40 years Together!

Now is the time to look back and forward.

I'm glad I married you because

I'm glad I married you because

You are both ten years older than you were when you wrote your last Family Mission. Even if that is the only thing that changed, it is time for a rewrite!

Our List of Big Changes

Updated Family Mission Statement

If there are additional family members, be sure to have them provide input toward the new mission. See your 30th Anniversary for your latest Family Mission Statement on page 121.

Our Forty-First
Anniversary

How we celebrated

The BEST memories of this year (events, trips, experiences):

Our goals for the coming year:

W A R M   T H O U G H T S

When I talk about you with my friends,

I tell them you are good at

Has what your partner is "good at" changed over the years? Write about that!

When I talk about you with my friends,

I tell them you are good at

Our Forty-Second
Anniversary

How we celebrated

The BEST memories of this year (events, trips, experiences):

What we learned about each other this year:

WARM THOUGHTS

If you were a tree you would be a _____

because

If you were a tree you would be a _____

because

Would it be a flowering tree or an evergreen? Would it be thorny? Would it live in a grove or stand solo? Is it ornamental?

Our Forty-Third
Anniversary

How we celebrated

The BEST memories of this year (events, trips, experiences):

What we learned about each other this year:

W A R M   T H O U G H T S

Thank you for doing _____

to make me feel better. It really mattered because

"Thank yous" matter so much! Don't let them slip away over time!

Thank you for doing _____

to make me feel better. It really mattered because

Our Forty-Fourth
Anniversary

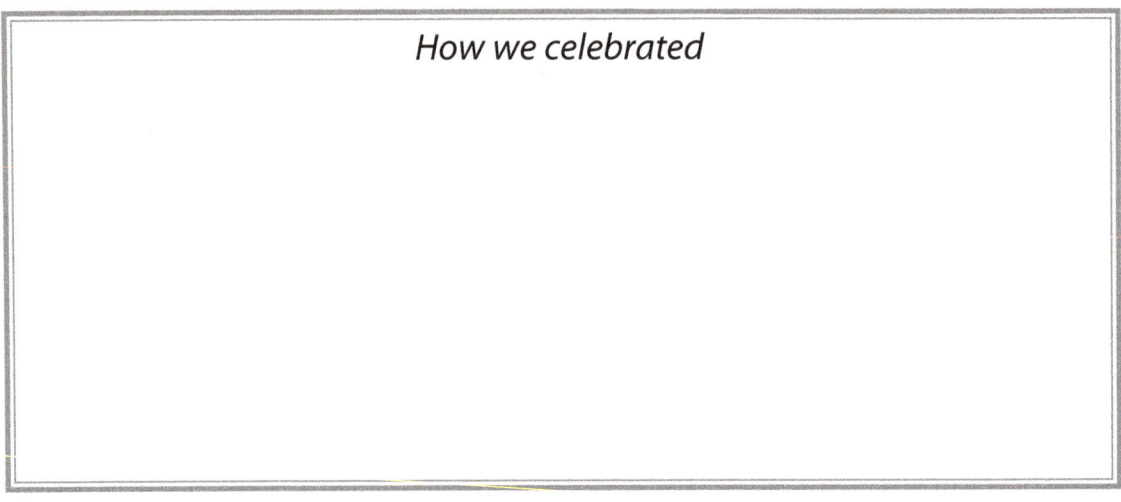

How we celebrated

The BEST memories of this year (events, trips, experiences):

What we learned about each other this year:

W A R M   T H O U G H T S

Thank you for teaching me to

Thank you for teaching me to

Learning from your partner helped you build your relationship. My dad taught my mom to drive.

If I could spend more time doing anything, I'd want that time to be with you.

Our Forty-Fifth
Anniversary

How we celebrated

The BEST memories of this year (events, trips, experiences):

What we learned about each other this year:

Our Forty-Fifth Anniversary

Our goals for the coming years:

Things we would like to do together:

How we would like to interact to enhance our relationship:

W A R M   T H O U G H T S

The song _____

always makes me think of you because

Is it the lyrics
or the tune?
Is it because of
an event or some
other reason?

The song _____

always makes me think of you because

Our Forty-Sixth
Anniversary

How we celebrated

The BEST memories of this year (events, trips, experiences):

What we learned about each other this year:

WARM THOUGHTS

My favorite nickname for you is

_____ *because*

Nicknames are a fun way to bond and make people smile. My cousin is warmly called "princesss" after three decades.

My favorite nickname for you is

_____ *because*

I call my husband "Boot" because he pulls off my cowboy boots.

Our Forty-Seventh
Anniversary

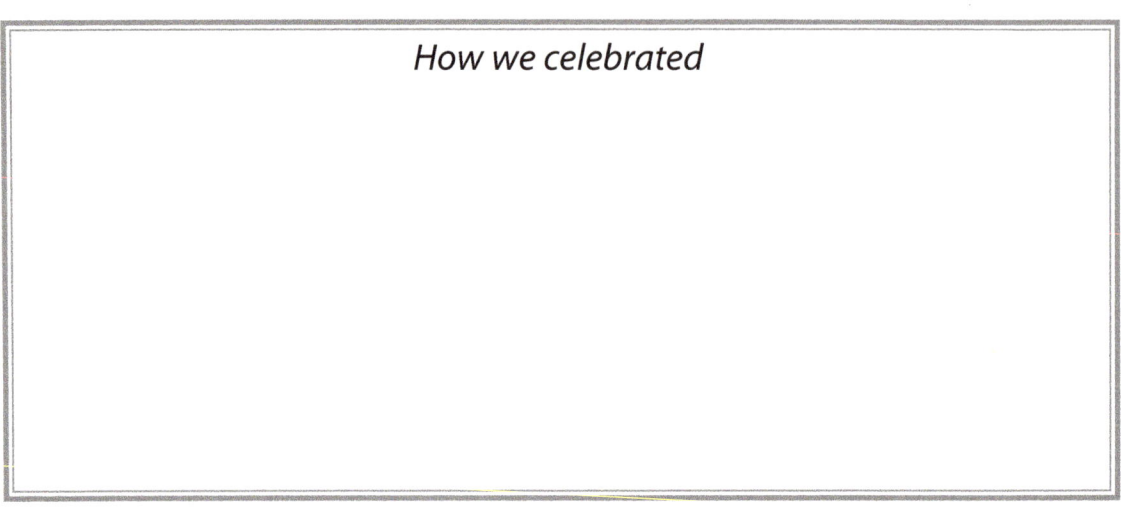

How we celebrated

The BEST memories of this year (events, trips, experiences):

What we learned about each other this year:

W A R M   T H O U G H T S

I wish more people had your _____

because

I wish more people had your _____

because

Is it their sense of humor or responsibility or perspective or faith? The list is endless.

Our Forty-Eighth
Anniversary

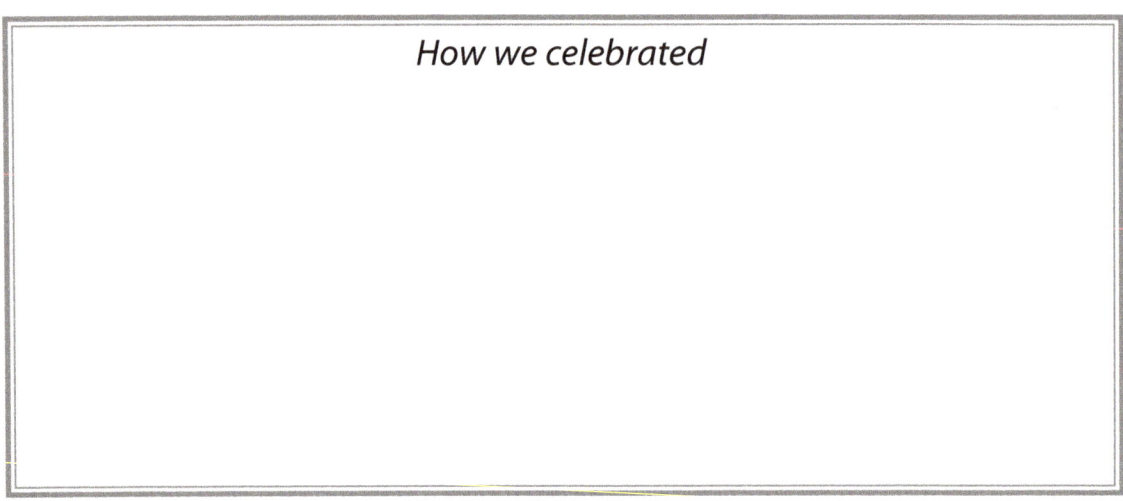

How we celebrated

The BEST memories of this year (events, trips, experiences):

What we learned about each other this year:

W A R M   T H O U G H T S

The hardest thing we did that helped

us to grow together was

The hardest thing we did that helped

us to grow together was

Hard moments can bond couples… if they focus on the solution.

Our Forty-Ninth
Anniversary

> *How we celebrated*

The BEST memories of this year (events, trips, experiences):

What we learned about each other this year:

WARM THOUGHTS

Thank you for helping me _____
because

Helping your partner is so important. It shows them you care. And saying thank you is equally important.

Thank you for helping me _____
because

When you smile at me across a room, I feel how much you love me.

Our Fiftieth
Anniversary

How we celebrated

The BEST memories of this year (events, trips, experiences):

What we learned about each other this year:

Our Fiftieth
Anniversary

Our goals for the coming year:

Things we would like to do together:

How we would like to interact to enhance our relationship:

W A R M T H O U G H T S

Big
Congratulations!
You have achieved
an amazing
accomplishment!

I have learned that the best way
to make you smile is to

I have learned that the best way
to make you smile is to

Be sure to share
with young couples
your thoughts and
perspectives about
a long, happy
relationship.

Congratulations
on 50 years Together!

Now is the time to look back and forward.

I'm glad we chose each other because

I'm glad we chose each other because

Our List of Big Changes

You are both ten years older than you were when you wrote your last Family Mission. Even if that is the only thing that changed, it is time for a rewrite!

Updated Family Mission Statement

If there are additional family members, be sure to have them provide input to the new mission. See your 40th Anniversary for your latest Family Mission Statement on page 147.

Our Journey Toward 70 Years Together

Our Fifty-First
Anniversary

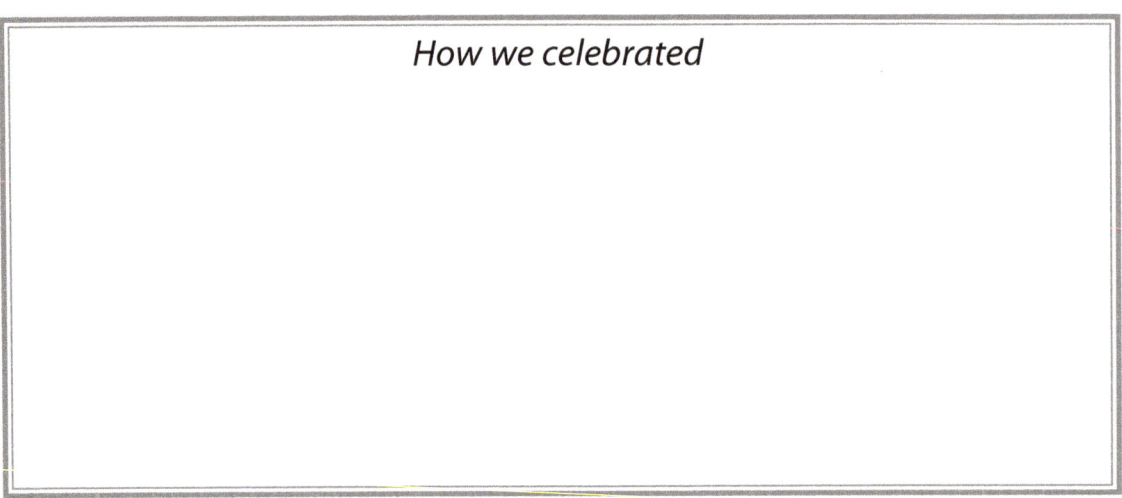

How we celebrated

The BEST memories of this year (events, trips, experiences):

What we learned about each other this year:

W A R M   T H O U G H T S

You showed your strength when you

Was it emotional strength, physical strength or financial planning/money management strength? Or was it something else?

You showed your strength when you

Our Fifty-Second
Anniversary

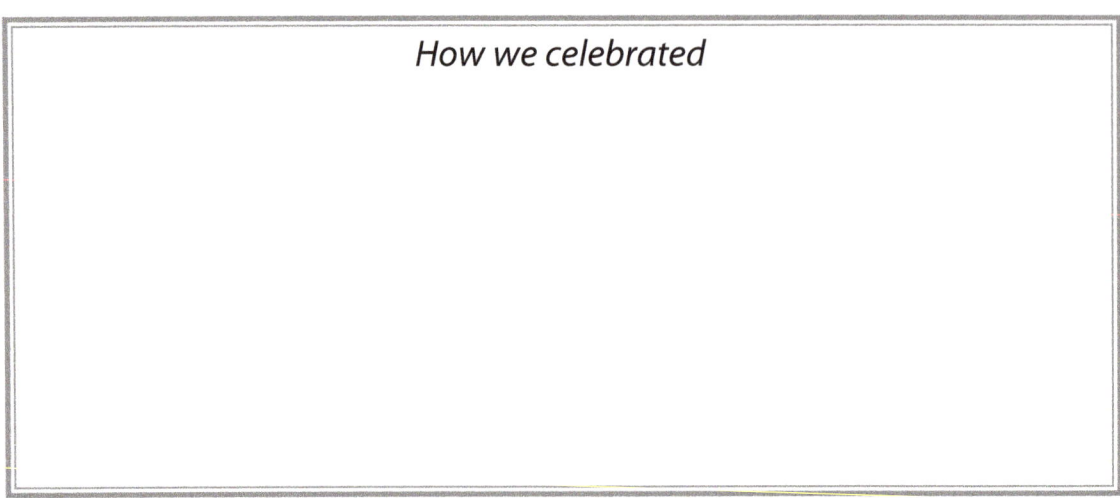

How we celebrated

The BEST memories of this year (events, trips, experiences):

What we learned about each other this year:

WARM THOUGHTS

If we could live a movie scene together,

I'd pick _____

from the movie _____ *because*

If we could live a movie scene together,

I'd pick _____

from the movie _____ *because*

Is it a western, a romantic comedy, an old movie or a cartoon?

Our Fifty-Third
Anniversary

How we celebrated

The BEST memories of this year (events, trips, experiences):

What we learned about each other this year:

WARM THOUGHTS

One of our favorite possessions is

_____ *because*

One of our favorite possessions is

_____ *because*

Consider how important the word "our" is here. Did you buy it together or inherit it? Or was it a gift?

Our Fifty-Fourth
Anniversary

How we celebrated

The BEST memories of this year (events, trips, experiences):

What we learned about each other this year:

WARM THOUGHTS

The best thing our relationship has taught me

Learning is a huge part of growing together. Is it patience or understanding, or something else?

The best thing our relationship has taught me

When I look at my entire life, I'm so glad you have been at the center.

Our Fifty-Fifth
Anniversary

How we celebrated

The BEST memories of this year (events, trips, experiences):

What we learned about each other this year:

Our Fifty-Fifth
Anniversary

Our goals for the coming years:

Things we would like to do together:

How we would like to interact to enhance our relationship:

WARM THOUGHTS

You would have been a great _____

because

You would have been a great _____

because

Our Fifty-Sixth
Anniversary

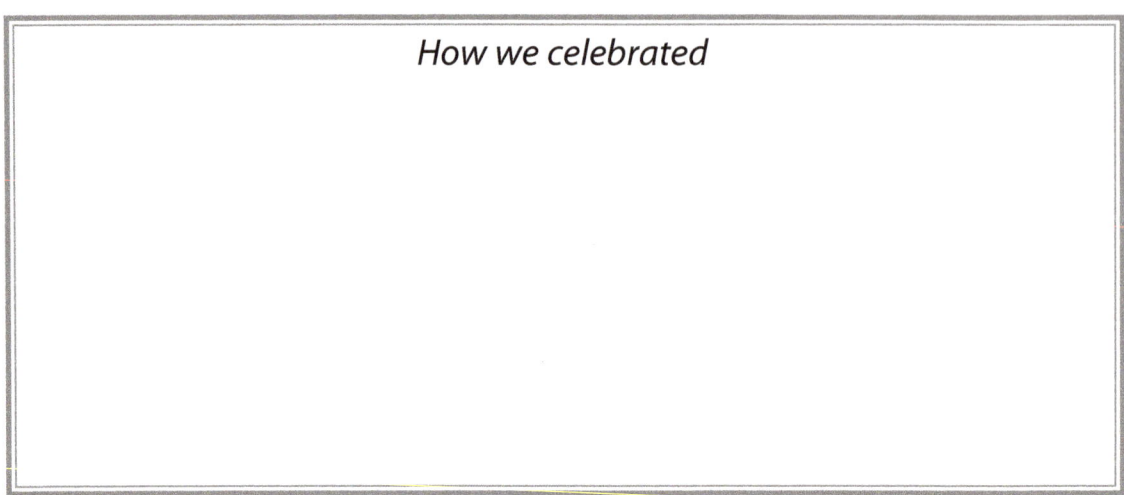

How we celebrated

The BEST memories of this year (events, trips, experiences):

What we learned about each other this year:

W A R M   T H O U G H T S

My favorite story about your childhood is

My favorite story about your childhood is

*T*he fact that you heard your partner's stories really matters. Which story about their childhood makes you smile?

Our Fifty-Seventh
Anniversary

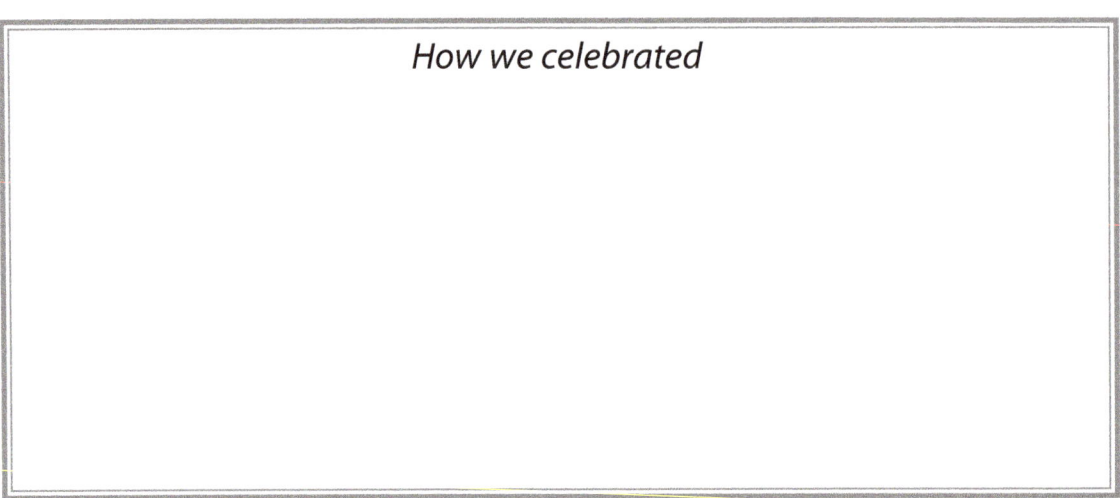

How we celebrated

The BEST memories of this year (events, trips, experiences):

What we learned about each other this year:

WARM THOUGHTS

The hardest I ever laughed was _____

because you

The hardest I ever laughed was _____

because you

Laughing with your partner is great! We hope this makes you laugh together again!

Our Fifty-Eighth
Anniversary

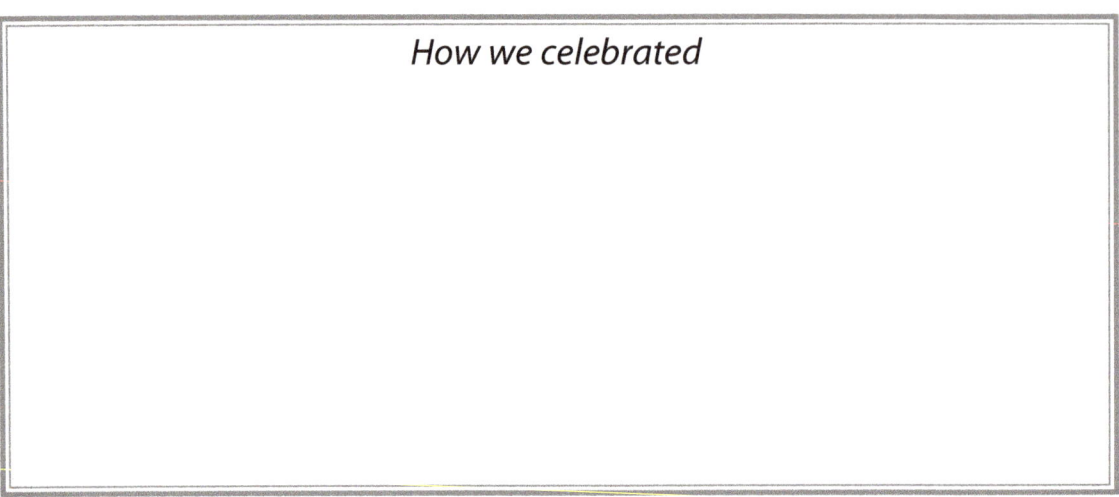

How we celebrated

The BEST memories of this year (events, trips, experiences):

What we learned about each other this year:

W A R M   T H O U G H T S

My fondest memory of when we first met is

Was it the time you first met or a few days later? Those first days together are special!

My fondest memory of when we first met is

Our Fifty-Ninth
Anniversary

How we celebrated

The BEST memories of this year (events, trips, experiences):

What we learned about each other this year:

W A R M   T H O U G H T S

My favorite anniversary was _____

because

My favorite anniversary was _____

because

*W*atch a movie
together – one
from the
"early years."

I love learning to do something new together.

Our Sixtieth
Anniversary

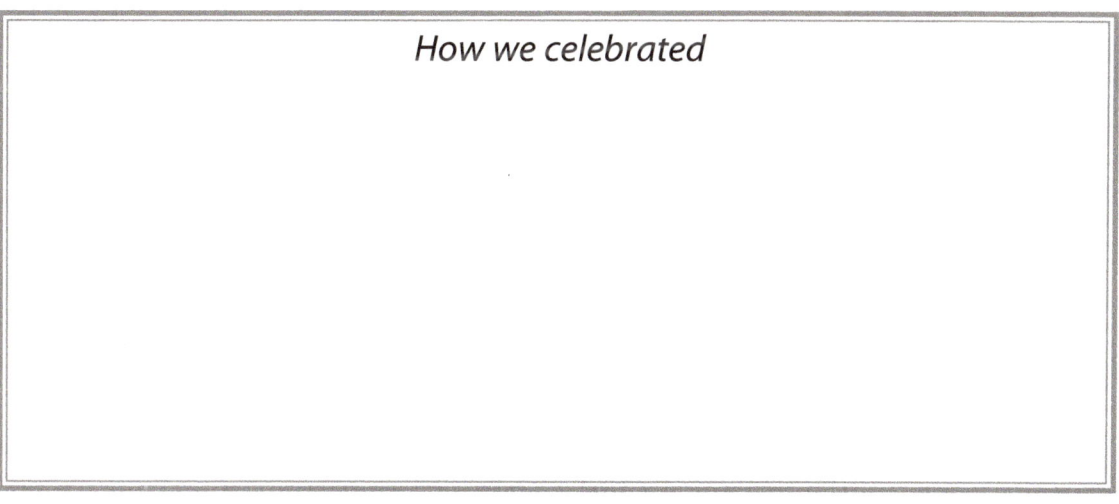

How we celebrated

The BEST memories of this year (events, trips, experiences):

What we learned about each other this year:

Our Sixtieth Anniversary

Our goals for the coming year:

Things we would like to do together:

How we would like to interact to enhance our relationship:

WARM THOUGHTS

My favorite birthday celebration was when we

Make birthdays special again this year!

My favorite birthday celebration was when we

Congratulations
on 60 years Together!

Now is the time to look back and forward.

I'm glad I chose to spend my life with you because

I'm glad I chose to spend my life with you because

You are both ten years older than you were when you wrote your last Family Mission. Even if that is the only thing that changed, it is time for a rewrite!

Our List of Big Changes

Updated Family Mission Statement

If there are additional family members, be sure to have them provide input to the new mission. See your 50th Anniversary for your latest Family Mission Statement on page 173.

Our Sixty-First
Anniversary

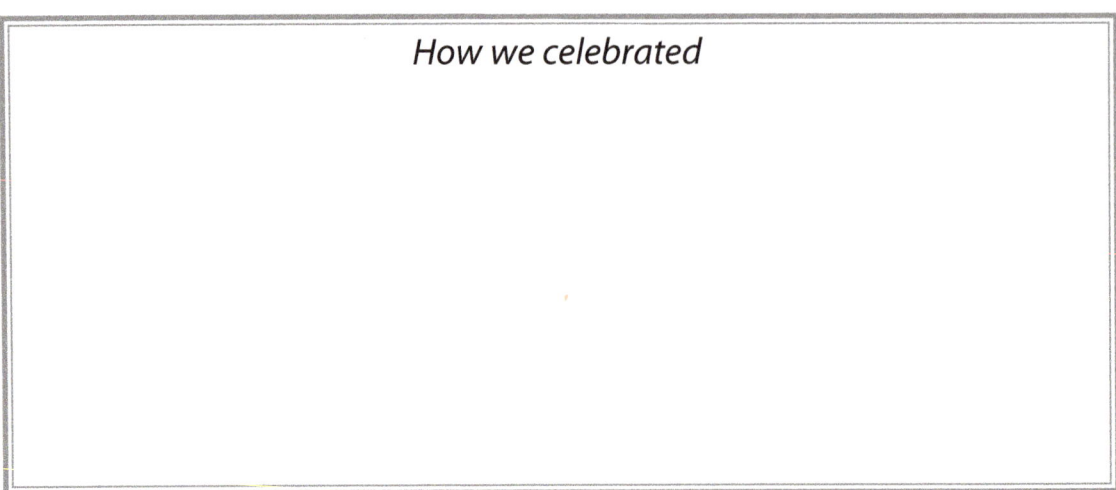

How we celebrated

The BEST memories of this year (events, trips, experiences):

What we learned about each other this year:

WARM THOUGHTS

I am so proud of how you have

You may find one big source of pride, or maybe you will hove a list of proud moments…

I am so proud of how you have

Our Sixty-Second
Anniversary

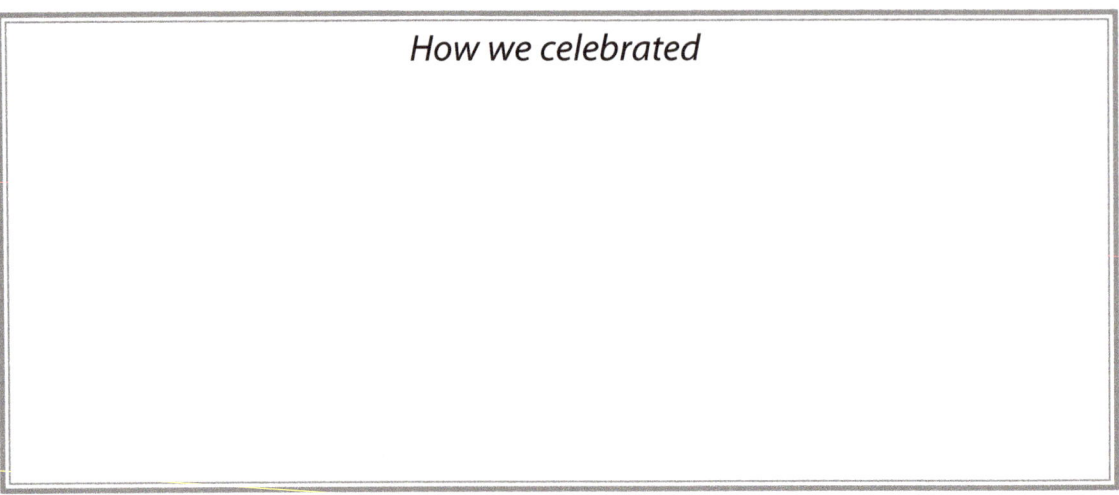

How we celebrated

The BEST memories of this year (events, trips, experiences):

What we learned about each other this year:

W A R M   T H O U G H T S

My favorite date with you was _____

in the early years, but today it is

My favorite date with you was _____

in the early years, but today it is

Recreate your favorite date from your early days. Plan it together – and grin as you remember your young selves.

Our Sixty-Third
Anniversary

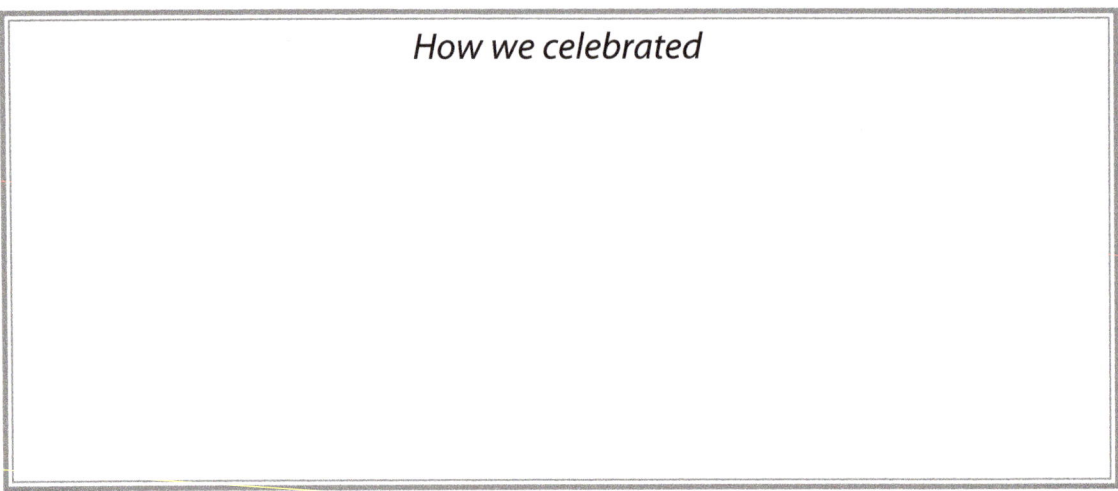

How we celebrated

The BEST memories of this year (events, trips, experiences):

What we learned about each other this year:

W A R M   T H O U G H T S

I missed you so much when

*W*as it recent or
from long ago?

I missed you so much when

Our Sixty-Fourth
Anniversary

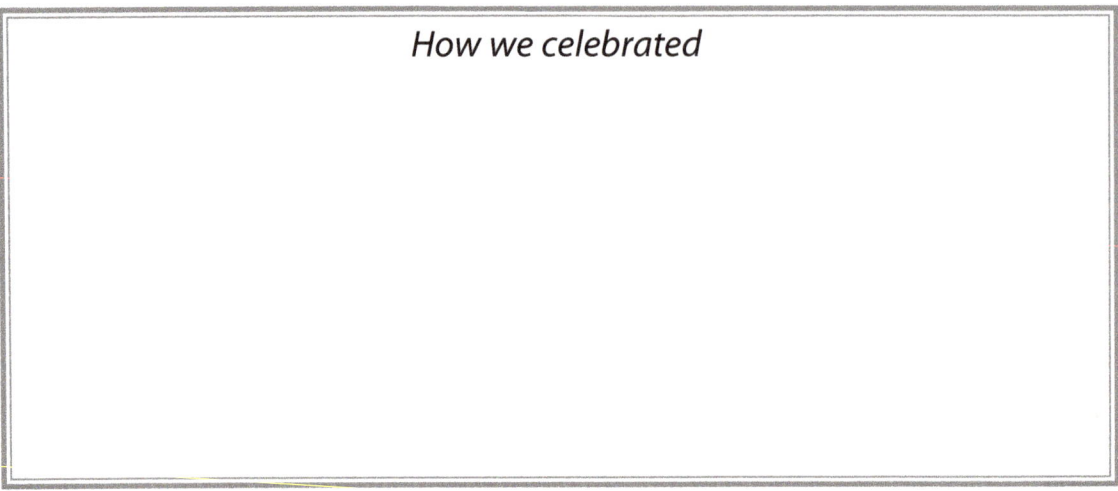

How we celebrated

The BEST memories of this year (events, trips, experiences):

What we learned about each other this year:

WARM THOUGHTS

We used to write notes on _____,

but now our notes are

Technology changes might make this interesting! Or maybe paper is still the best place to write a note!

We used to write notes on _____,

but now our notes are

Holding your hand brings me a sense of calm.

Our Sixty-Fifth
Anniversary

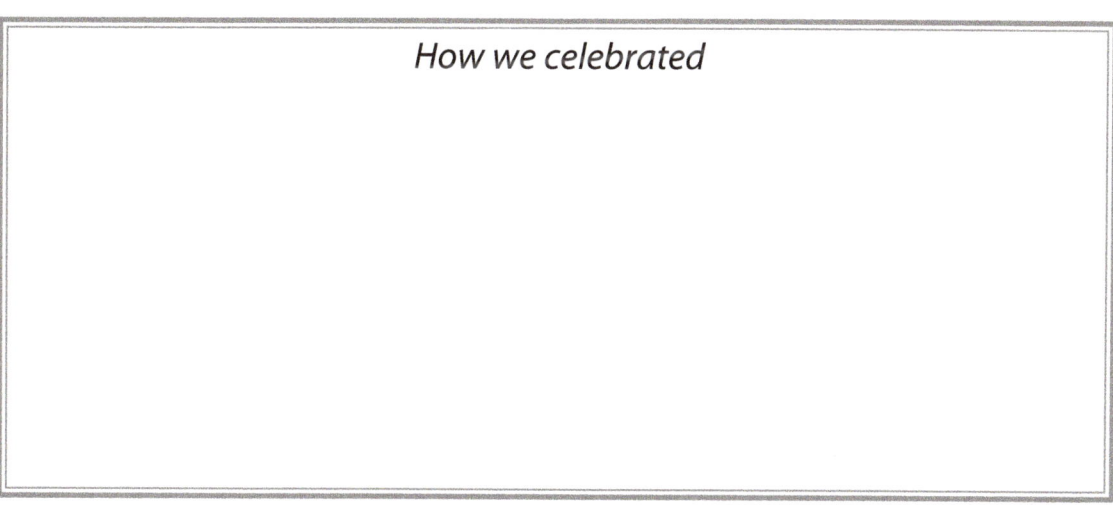

How we celebrated

The BEST memories of this year (events, trips, experiences):

What we learned about each other this year:

Our Sixty-Fifth
Anniversary

Our goals for the coming year:

Things we would like to do together:

How we would like to interact to enhance our relationship:

WARM THOUGHTS

When I want to smile, I remember our

Your life together is filled with memories. What makes you smile?

When I want to smile, I remember our

Our Sixty-Sixth
Anniversary

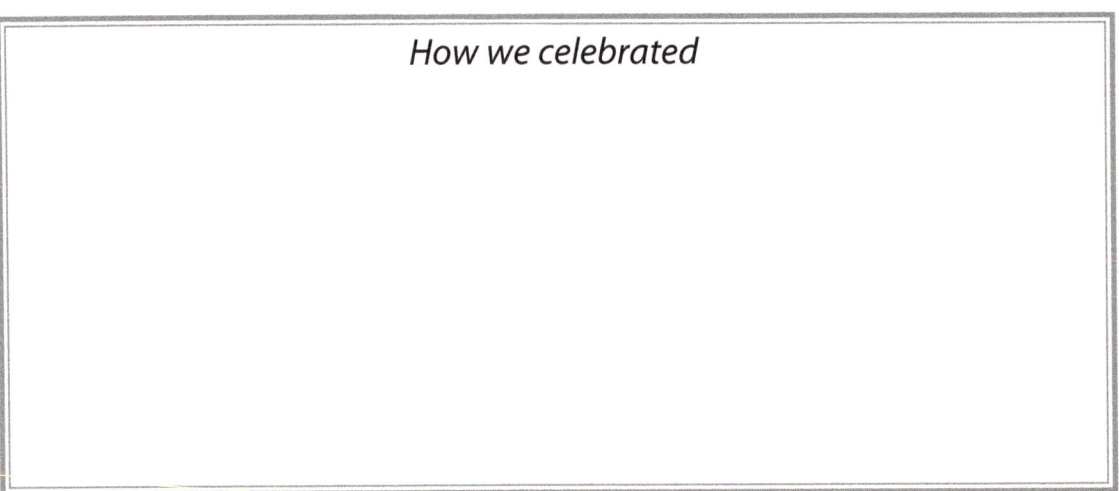

How we celebrated

The BEST memories of this year (events, trips, experiences):

What we learned about each other this year:

WARM THOUGHTS

I love remembering the sound of _____

on our trip to

Was it a creek or rain or waves? Or leaves blowing or children laughing? Music or just quiet?

I love remembering the sound of _____

on our trip to

Our Sixty-Seventh
Anniversary

How we celebrated

The BEST memories of this year (events, trips, experiences):

What we learned about each other this year:

WARM THOUGHTS

The best gift you have ever given me is

The best gift you have ever given me is

*B*ring flowers
home! Or cut some
from the garden.

Our Sixty-Eighth
Anniversary

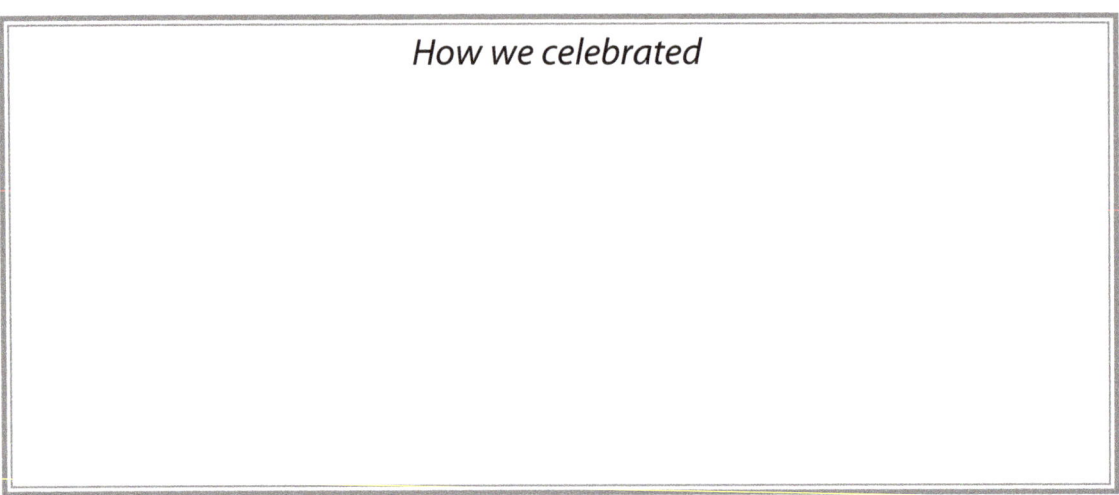

How we celebrated

The BEST memories of this year (events, trips, experiences):

What we learned about each other this year:

W A R M   T H O U G H T S

When I want to relax, I remember our

Long talks, quiet walks, warm hugs?

When I want to relax, I remember our

Our Sixty-Ninth
Anniversary

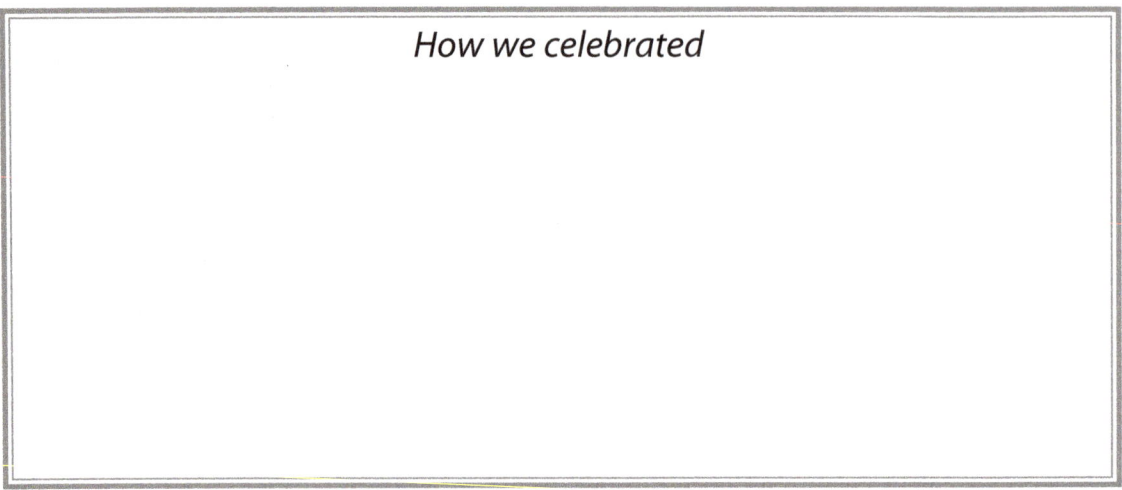

How we celebrated

The BEST memories of this year (events, trips, experiences):

What we learned about each other this year:

W A R M   T H O U G H T S

I am so glad that together we were

able to accomplish

Your wonderful life together is an accomplishment. What key pieces helped make it special?

I am so glad that together we were

able to accomplish

CHAPTER

Seven

Thoughts About Our Life Together

The best part of me knows the best part of you.

Our Seventieth
Anniversary

How we celebrated

The BEST memories of this year (events, trips, experiences):

What we learned about each other this year:

Our Seventieth
Anniversary

Our goals for the coming year:

Things we would like to do together:

How we would like to interact to enhance our relationship:

WARM THOUGHTS

When I want to explain the best part of our relationship to someone younger, I tell them about

Share your wisdom! Give them courage and confidence.!

When I want to explain the best part of our relationship to someone younger, I tell them about

Thoughts About Our Life Together

_____

_____

_____

_____

_____

_____

_____

_____

_____

_____

_____

Thoughts About Our Life Together

_____

_____

_____

_____

_____

_____

_____

_____

_____

_____

_____

Thoughts About Our Life Together

_____

_____

_____

_____

_____

_____

_____

_____

_____

_____

_____

Thoughts About Our Life Together

_____

_____

_____

_____

_____

_____

_____

_____

_____

_____

Thoughts About Our Life Together

_____

_____

_____

_____

_____

_____

_____

_____

_____

_____

CPSIA information can be obtained
at www.ICGtesting.com
Printed in the USA
BVHW050824061221
620397BV00008B/35